First Published in the UK in September 2010 by Focus Education (UK) Ltd
Updated in January 2012
Updated in September 2013
Updated September 2014

Focus Education (UK) Ltd
Talking Point Conference and Exhibition Centre
Huddersfield Road
Scouthead
Saddleworth
OL4 4AG

Focus Education (UK) Ltd Reg. No 4507968

ISBN 978-1-904469-81-0

Companies, institutions and other organisations wishing to make bulk purchases of books published by Focus Education should contact their local bookstore or Focus Education direct:

Customer Services, Focus Education, Talking Point Conference and Exhibition Centre,
Huddersfield Road, Scouthead, Saddleworth, OL4 4AG
Tel 01457 821818 Fax 01457 878205

www.focus-education.co.uk
customerservice@focus-education.co.uk
Printed in Great Britain by Focus Education UK Ltd, Scouthead

Users should be fully aware that Ofsted may change any element of their guidance.
This document was wholly accurate at the date of publication.

About the author

Simon Camby is the Chief Executive of the Focus Academy Trust. Prior to this, Simon was a Director at Focus Education.

Simon has a well-established track record in education which includes work as a headteacher, senior local authority adviser and lead Ofsted inspector. The inspection in his most recent headship acknowledged:

- *'The headteacher has the respect of the local community and, as a result, parents are overwhelmingly supportive of the school.'*
- *'The determination of the headteacher and leadership team to enhance the pupils' quality of education is in evidence throughout the school and provides the inspiration from which all staff gain strength.'*
- *His strong and inspirational leadership provides clear educational direction, as a result rapid progress has been made in addressing the many weaknesses identified at the time of the last inspection.'*

Simon has written a wide range of publications which adopt a clear and user-friendly style.

Simon is well established as a consultant and his work is highly valued by school and LA leaders both in England and overseas. His main areas of work link to quality leadership, improving learning, quality assessment and curriculum innovation. He works with colleagues in school to help drive their improvements as well as leading conferences and training across England and with international schools. Simon also has a small number of clients who he works with as a leadership coach. He is an accredited Myers Briggs (MBTI) practitioner and uses this as a tool in leadership coaching and leadership team development work. Simon has undertaken Ofsted inspection training and inspects under the current framework.

Recent feedback from delegates who attended training led by Simon notes:

- *'The best training I have ever attended.'* (Primary head)
- *'Everyone commented on the quality of the training. Everyone felt confident to contribute. We are totally fired up! Thank you.'* (Infant head)
- *'Simon broke everything down so that it made perfect sense. I have so many practical tools that can be used straight away.'* (Teacher)
- *'Wow! Once again a fantastic, provoking and brilliant day. The staff feel reinvigorated. Thank you.'* (Headteacher)
- *'Highly professional in approach. Managed the needs of the diverse audience superbly.'* (LA Head of School Improvement)

Contents

Introduction

Introduction

Whilst safeguarding will be evaluated in its own right when a school is inspected, it will also be considered in relation to its impact on other aspects of the inspection framework, e.g. pupil outcomes, tracking of vulnerable pupils, equality of opportunity, curricular provision, leadership and management, etc. It is important that schools can demonstrate that safeguarding extends beyond paper-based and electronic systems, and that it impacts on the provision and outcomes for children and young people. The most effective schools will be able to correlate their approach to safeguarding with their success in ensuring that children are safe and achieve.

This document focuses mainly on systems in place as a measurable check for school leaders. However, leaders need to be able to demonstrate that the curriculum (both explicit and implicit) places a high priority on safeguarding and being safe. This will ultimately be tested through ensuring that pupils feel safe. In addition, school leaders should be aware that this document does not focus on the elements of safeguarding connected with health and safety issues.

This safeguarding audit tool is designed to help school leaders evaluate whether they meet requirements which will be tested out through inspection. In assessing, leaders will gather powerful evidence for their self-evaluation summary statement and for reporting to governors.

It is intended to be used to make headline checks. Outcomes from these checks will enable leaders to drill down, if deeper investigation is required. The audits outline statutory requirements and also include some elements of best practice which go further than the actual legislation.

It has been designed with the intention that school leaders will use it selectively in order to access the sections which will help them most.

Completion of this record will provide valuable evidence that a rigorous evaluation of safeguarding systems has taken place thus demonstrating its importance to the school. The audits are included as word documents so that it is easy to personalise and update them.

It is recommended that this audit is completed collectively by all staff with safeguarding responsibilities. This type of approach will ensure a reminder of the requirements and mean that any member of this team could discuss the school's approach to safeguarding with an inspector or external evaluator. Many schools find it useful to involve a governor with this process.

Key documents

Staff with safeguarding responsibilities should read these documents.

Department
for Education

Keeping children safe in education

Statutory guidance for schools and colleges

April 2014

HM Government

Working Together to Safeguard Children

A guide to inter-agency working to safeguard and promote the welfare of children

March 2013

What is safeguarding?

- Protecting children from maltreatment.

- Preventing impairment of children's health or development.

- Ensuring that children are growing up in circumstances consistent with the provision of safe and effective care.

- Taking action to enable all children to have the best outcomes.

[Children Act 2004]

Key questions

Key questions

- Do children know how to raise concerns?
- Can they name people they would talk to?
- Do they feel that their concerns would be heard?
- Can children give examples of times when adults have listened and helped?

- Do adults know about the child protection policy?
- Have they had training and briefings?
- Do they know who the Designated Safeguarding Lead (DSL) is?

- Is it clear who the Designated Safeguarding Lead is? Is this documented?

- Are written records clear and securely stored?
- Is there evidence that appropriate referrals have been made to Social Care and/or external agencies? Is this documented?
- Is there evidence of plans in place to protect children?

- Is there evidence that the school follows the agreed procedures for children missing from education?

Key questions

- Are risk assessments in place?
- Can the school evidence ways in which it teaches children about managing risk?

- Are there clear procedures in place for implementation of the agreed behaviour policy?
- Are records in place which show how restraint has been implemented?

- Can children talk about the school's work on dealing with discrimination?
- Can children talk about the school's work to help them be safe online or when using technology?

- Are there clear selection and vetting procedures in place?

- Are there clear records evidencing child protection training?

- Does the school have clearly publicised systems which help people to make a complaint or whistle blow?

Safeguarding does not stand in isolation

Safeguarding does not stand in isolation

Your safeguarding policy and procedures are linked to many other policies and documents. The following are the obvious links:

- Child protection policy
- Health and safety policy and handbook
- Discipline policy (including sanctions, rewards and restraint)
- Staff disciplinary, grievance and whistleblowing policies
- Use of reasonable force policy
- Meeting the needs of medical conditions of pupils guidance
- First aid policy
- Educational visits policy
- Intimate care policy
- E-safety policy
- Site security policy, including access to school premises outside school hours
- Staff Handbook
- Staff Code of Conduct
- Complaints procedure
- Emergency planning arrangements
- Staff induction arrangements, including training and development programme
- Job descriptions

Safeguarding does not stand in isolation

Your safeguarding arrangements link to a range of other issues which will be addressed through PSHE, safeguarding and behaviour policies, guidance and work:

- Bullying (incl cyber bullying and prejudice based bullying)
- Racist, disability, and homophobic or transphobic abuse
- Radicalisation and extremist behaviour
- Attendance and punctuality
- Child sexual exploitation
- Sexting
- Substance misuse
- Gang activity and youth violence
- Domestic violence
- Female genital mutilation
- Forced marriage.

Documentation audit linked to safeguarding

Policy/Procedure/ Document	Notes	In place	Not in place	Person/s responsible	Deadline/ Review date
Action plan (following inspection or external review)	Address any issues relating to safeguarding.				
Attendance policy	Includes reference to safeguarding.				
Child protection	Detailed procedure familiar to all staff, governors and volunteers – all of whom have a copy. Include reference to transition arrangements and transfer of intelligence and documentation.				
Child protection (information for parents)	Provide summary information for parents about school responsibility for child protection and safeguarding.				
Complaints	Head, senior leaders, chair of governors, vice chair all understand and ready to implement.				
Confidentiality	Include reference to how this contributes to safeguarding.				

Policy/Procedure/ Document	Notes	In place	Not in place	Person/s responsible	Deadline/ Review date
Curriculum	Include reference to ways the curriculum contributes to safeguarding.				
Discipline (including anti-bullying)	Include reference to measures made to safeguarding children (may also cross reference to Policy on use of force to control or restrain pupils). Include reference to racist incidents, homophobic bullying, harassment and discrimination.				
Drug and substance	Include reference to how this contributes to safeguarding.				
Educational visits	Include reference to safeguarding children.				
E-safety	Include reference to systems and procedures. May link to acceptable use policy.				
First aid (including administration of medicine)	Include details of first aiders, dates of training, protocols, input from external agencies.				
Governing body and committee papers	Evidence review and evaluation of safeguarding procedures and relevant actions.				

Policy/Procedure/ Document	Notes	In place	Not in place	Person/s responsible	Deadline/ Review date
Health and safety (Including policy and recent inspection reports & action plans)	Include measures taken to safeguard pupils.				
Home-School agreement	Include reference to safeguarding.				
Intimate care	Include measures taken to safeguard pupils and how this is shared with parents/carers.				
Internet and e-safety	Include clear rules regarding what is permissible for staff and pupils, including pupil supervision arrangements. Include code of conduct to be signed by parents.				
Images of children (use of)	Include protocols for using and displaying photographs, including use in internal and external publications. Include details about parent/carer consent.				
Meeting the needs of children with medical conditions	Clear guidance about how needs are met				
Prospectus/website	Include reference to school's duties and procedures regarding safeguarding and child protection; include name(s) of designated staff.				

Policy/Procedure/ Document	Notes	In place	Not in place	Person/s responsible	Deadline/ Review date
Race equality	Include measures taken for safeguarding children.				
Risk assessments	Include measures taken for safeguarding children; evidence of clear procedures and record keeping system.				
Safe working practices (for the protection of children and staff in education settings)	Refers to established boundaries in place to protect all stakeholders and pupils.				
Safer recruitment	Includes reference to safeguarding and legal responsibilities. Includes details of checks undertaken before appointment.				
School security	Include details of security systems to safeguard, protocol for emergencies, management of visitors on site.				
Sex and relationships	Include reference to how this contributes to safeguarding.				

Policy/Procedure/ Document	Notes	In place	Not in place	Person/s responsible	Deadline/ Review date
Special educational needs/disabilities	Include reference to safeguarding pupils; particularly identifying issues for vulnerable pupils.				
Staff code of conduct	Include explicit expectations about code of behaviour for staff.				
Staff discipline, conduct and grievance	Refer to procedures that must be followed if allegations of abuse are made against a member of staff.				
Use of force to control or restrain pupils	Include clear procedures based on DFE guidance; include clear recording system.				
Volunteers and occasional visitors	Include details about measures taken to safeguard pupils.				
Whistle blowing	Clear information for staff on steps to take if they have concerns about a person working at the school.				

Note that the above list does not imply that all these documents are statutory.
Refer to the 'Governors Guide to the Law' for a list of statutory policies in maintained schools.

Child protection audit

Strand	Point to check	Evidence	Actions (if necessary)
Child Protection	Child protection policy in place and reviewed annually.		
	Evidence of staff briefings on policy.		
	All staff have a copy of the policy.		
	Appropriate briefings and information provided for visitors and volunteers, including written documentation.		
	Statement about safeguarding and child protection communicated to parents and carers.		
	Clear reference to child protection and safeguarding in staff handbook.		
	Clear signage in key areas identifying names of designated staff.		
	Evidence of monitoring and evaluation of policy; including at governor level.		

Strands	Point to check	Evidence	Actions (if necessary)
Designated Staff	Correct number of designated staff (inc. member of leadership team).		
Training	Training record in place for designated staff.		
	Training record in place for whole staff.		
	Evidence of training on inter-agency and partnership working to safeguard pupils.		
	Safeguarding and child protection included in induction arrangements for all groups of staff.		
	Appropriate training and information for temporary staff.		
	Appropriate training for volunteers.		
	Staff with responsibility for attendance trained on link between attendance and safeguarding.		
	At least one person on each recruitment panel undertaken safer recruitment training.		

Strand	Point to check	Evidence	Actions (if necessary)
Record Keeping	Stored securely with controlled access.		
	Up to date and complete.		
	Evidence of clear and transparent records, i.e. can they be easily followed by someone else?		
	Records show effective identification and management of risk of harm.		
	Evidence of sound decision making, appropriate responses and timely referrals.		
	Evidence that concerns were well followed up to safeguard pupils.		
	Evidence of work with other agencies.		
	Evidence of work with parents/carers.		
	Evidence of information sharing, including inter-agency meetings and case conferences.		
	Clear procedure for transfer of information when pupil leaves the school.		

Responsibilities on governing bodies and proprietors

Key responsibilities

The following pages outline the key responsibilities placed on governing bodies and proprietors to comply with their safeguarding duties under legislation.

These pages can be used as a simple audit to check that the appropriate procedures are in place to evidence compliance.

Responsibilities placed on governing bodies and proprietors include:		
	Compliant?	**Actions?**
Can you evidence inter-agency working? (Including providing a coordinated offer of early help when additional needs of children are identified.)		
Can you evidence that an effective child protection policy is in place?		
Can you evidence that an effective staff code of conduct/staff behaviour policy is in place?		
Can you evidence that you have a Designated Safeguarding Lead who has been trained every two years?		
Can you evidence that the DSL has a specific outline for this role in their job description?		
Can you evidence that all staff have read the 8-page summary in 'Keeping Children Safe in Education' (2014)?		
Can you evidence that you have a designated teacher to promote the educational achievement of looked after children?		
Can you evidence that children are taught about how to keep themselves safe?		

Responsibilities placed on governing bodies and proprietors include:		
	Compliant?	Actions?
Can you evidence that you adhere to your statutory responsibilities in vetting adults that work with children?		
Can you evidence that you risk assess and take proportionate decisions on whether to ask for checks beyond that which is required?		
Can you evidence that you ensure that volunteers are appropriately supervised?		
Can you evidence that at least one person on each appointment panel has undertaken safer recruitment training?		
Can you evidence that you have procedures in place to handle allegations against staff and volunteers?		
Can you evidence that you have procedures in place to handle allegations against other children?		
Can you evidence that you know what the procedures are to deal with pupils who go missing from education? Can you evidence that you have used these?		

Single central record

Single central record

Your school's single central record must be kept constantly up to date.

Many schools now ask a governor to do some spot checks throughout the year in order to test out the single central record.

The chart on the following page gives you some pointers to evaluate your SCR.

	Fully in place	Partly in place	Not in place
Names			
Address (include date seen and initials of person who saw it)			
DOB			
Identity check (include date seen and initials of person who saw it)			
Start date			
Role			
Whether they need **qualifications** for the role Y/N			
(If relevant) which **qualifications** seen, date seen and who checked			
Prohibited list/Barred list (include date and who checked)			
CRB/DBS number			
CRB/DBS (who saw the disclosure and date)			
Right to work in UK (indicate date seen and who checked)			
Overseas check (whether required Y/N)			
Overseas check (indicate date checks complete and who completed)			
Evidence of checks in place for supply staff			
Evidence of checks in place for peripatetic staff			
Evidence of checks in place for sub contracted staff			
Evidence of checks in place for governors (if required)			

Ofsted and safeguarding

Ofsted and safeguarding

Ofsted look at safeguarding through different aspects of the Ofsted Evaluation Schedule:

Leadership and management	Behaviour and safety
Inspectors should consider the effectiveness of safeguarding arrangements to ensure that there is safe recruitment and that all pupils are safe. This includes the: • maintenance of the single central record and appropriate arrangements for child protection • rigour with which pupil absence is followed up, including appropriate checks when pupils cease attending • effectiveness with which a school identified any pupils who may be at risk, using a case study approach based on concerns about individual pupils that may have originated either inside or outside the school • decision-making processes involved in taking pupils off roll • actions taken following any serious incident • effectiveness of the arrangements for safeguarding pupils who are educated wholly or partly off-site at a unit run by the school or at alternative provision • approach to keeping pupils safe from the dangers of radicalisation and extremism, and what is done when it is suspected that pupils are vulnerable to these • promotion of safe practice and a culture of safety, including e-safety.	Inspectors should consider: • the success in keeping pupils safe, whether within school or during external activities through, for instance, effective risk assessments, e-safety arrangements and action taken following any serious safeguarding incident • the school's policy and procedures for ensuring that visitors to the school are suitably checked and monitored as appropriate, for example external speakers at school assemblies. (See Evaluation Schedule for full list of wider areas to check within Behaviour and Safety)

Ofsted and safeguarding

	Outstanding	Good	Inadequate
Extract from descriptors for leadership and management	The school is adept at identifying any child at risk of harm and engaging with partners to respond appropriately. Staff model professional standards in all of their work and demonstrate high levels of respect and courtesy for pupils and others.	Leaders ensure that staff are well trained in identifying pupils at risk of harm and responding appropriately. The school's arrangements for safeguarding pupils meet statutory requirements.	The school's arrangements for safeguarding pupils do not meet statutory requirements and give serious cause for concern, or insufficient action has been taken to remedy weaknesses following a serious incident. The school fails to identify pupils at risk of harm when it might reasonably have done so.
Extract from descriptors for leadership and management	All groups of pupils are safe and feel safe in school and at alternative provision placements at all times. They understand very clearly what constitutes unsafe situations and are highly aware of how to keep themselves and others safe in different situations, including in relation to e-safety.	Pupils are safe and feel safe in school and at alternative provision placements; they understand how to keep themselves safe in different situations.	Pupils or particular groups of pupils are not safe or do not feel safe at school and/or at alternative placements.

Auditing E-safety

Auditing e-safety

The following pages may be of use when undertaking an evaluation of e-safety in your school. The charts identify Ofsted key features of good and outstanding practice alongside examples of what this could look like in school. The chart below outlined possible questions which inspectors may use when talking to children and staff.

Questions for children	Questions for staff
<ul><li>If you felt uncomfortable about anything you saw, or if anybody asked you for your personal details, would you know where to go for help?</li><li>If anybody sent you hurtful messages on the internet or on your mobile phone would you know who to tell?</li><li>Can you tell me the rules that your school has for using the internet?</li><li>How do you keep yourself safe online?</li><li>Do you understand what the risks of posting inappropriate content on the internet are? (secondary students)</li></ul>	<ul><li>Have you had any training specifically about e-safety?</li><li>How is e-safety addressed through the curriculum? What has been the impact?</li><li>What policies and procedures are in place to ensure good e-safety for all staff and pupils?</li><li>What sanctions are in place to enforce these?</li><li>How confident are you that cyber bullying is understood and addressed in school?</li><li>What reporting mechanisms are in place for pupils who feel they may be subject to cyber bullying?</li><li>How well do all staff share the responsibility for e-safety?</li><li>What do you do, as a school, to work with parents and carers on e-safety as a priority?</li></ul>

	Key features of good and outstanding practice	What might this look like?	Your self-evaluation and next steps…
Whole-school consistent approach	All teaching and support staff can recognise and are aware of e-safety issues.	E-safety policy is included in induction pack for all new staff. Regular (at least annual) training for all staff. At least one member of staff has accredited training, e.g. CEOP, EPICT.	
	High quality leadership and management make e-safety a priority across all areas of the school.	The school has achieved a recognised standard, e.g. e-safety mark.	
	A high priority given to training in e-safety, extending expertise widely and building internal capacity.	Quality training based on individual needs assessment as well as whole-school approach.	
	The contribution of pupils, parents and the wider school community is valued and integrated.	E-safety issues discussed with school council, e-safety ambassadors, governors, parents via questionnaires and their views incorporated in school policy.	

	Key features of good and outstanding practice	What might this look like?	Your self-evaluation and next steps…
Robust & integrated reporting routines	School-based online reporting processes that are clearly understood by the whole school, allowing the pupils to report issues to nominated staff. Report abuse buttons.	For example, SHARP, Dolphin etc. For example, CEOP.	
Policies	Rigorous e-safety policies and procedures are in place, written in plain English, contributed to by the whole school, updated regularly and ratified by governors.	Policy is reviewed annually and addresses any relevant developments in ICT.	
	Policies understood by staff.	All staff required to sign e-safety policy.	
	E-safety policy should incorporate an Acceptable Usage Policy that is signed by pupils and/or parents as well as staff and respected by all.	Acceptable Usage Policy returned for all pupil. Arrangements in place to follow up any non-returns.	

	Key features of good and outstanding practice	What might this look like?	Your self-evaluation and next steps...
Education	A progressive curriculum that is flexible, relevant and engages pupils interest; that is used to promote e-safety through teaching pupils how to stay safe, how to protect themselves from harm and how to take responsibility for their own and others safe.	Clear identification of e-safety 'journey' for all pupils from entry into younger cohort through to leaving the school. E-safety curriculum is reviewed annually to respond to developments in ICT.	
	Positive sanctions are used to reward positive and responsible use.	Pupils can clearly explain rewards and sanctions.	
	Peer mentoring programmes.	May be older pupils working with peers or younger pupils but also possibly for pupils who join other than at usual age of entry.	
Infrastructure	Recognised internet service provider together with age related filtering that is actively monitored.	Filtering system updated regularly and with clearly systems for reporting any breaches.	
Monitoring and evaluation	Risk assessment taken seriously and used to good effect in promoting e-safety.	Staff aware of relevant risk assessments and can link content to their classroom practice.	
	Using data effectively to assess the impact of e-safety practice and how this informs strategy.	School survey of pupils and parents includes collecting data on use of mobile phones and/or social networking by pupils. Impact of e-safety assessed via pupil voice	

Evaluating safeguarding in your school

Self-evaluation of safeguarding

The charts on the following pages are intended to help you structure a simple way to evaluate safeguarding within your school.

They are not exhaustive and there may be other aspects that are particular to your context that you may wish to include.

For each aspect - consider:

Judgement	Evidence	Next step/s
▪ *Is it good enough?* ▪ *How would you grade it?*	▪ *How do you know?* ▪ *How can you back up your judgment?*	▪ *What do you need to do in order to bring about improvement?*

	Judgement	Evidence	Next step/s
Child protection arrangements			
Child protection policy in place and communicated			
Child protection records in place and securely stored			
DSL in place, trained and all staff know who it is			

	Judgement	Evidence	Next step/s
Robust recruitment			
Robust vetting			
Induction procedures			
Training and information sharing			

	Judgement	Evidence	Next step/s
Clarity of roles and responsibilities			
Policies & procedures (linked to safeguarding)			
Risk assessments			
Teaching about how to manage risk in the curriculum			

	Judgement	Evidence	Next step/s
Single central record			
Complaint and whistleblowing procedure			
Children feel safe			

Safer recruitment

Safer recruitment

The purpose of this section is to outline the steps that you need to take in order to ensure that you have a robust safer recruitment process in place.

You may wish to review your existing process in order to check out each of the steps. You may, of course, go beyond these requirements.

These notes have been compiled from a variety of sources outlining best practice and provide background to the safer recruitment audit.

BEFORE DETAILS OF POST ARE RELEASED

Step 1: **Policy**	Up to date recruitment and selection policy in place.
Step 2: **Safer recruitment commitment**	Commitment to safer recruitment commitment included on relevant documents: • publicity materials; • advertisements and recruitment websites; • candidate information packs; • job descriptions, person specifications and competency frameworks ; • induction training and probation arrangements. All personnel involved in recruitment have received appropriate <u>training</u>.

BEFORE DETAILS OF POST ARE RELEASED

Step 3: **Process planning, including job description and person spec**	Organise the timetable for the recruitment process to allow references to be obtained on short-listed candidates before interview. Job descriptions should be completed in a consistent template for the organisation and should clearly state: • the title of the post; • the location and/or department in which the post is based; • the position to which the post reports; • positions (if any) or numbers of staff for which the post is responsible; • the salary and/or grade within which the post is located; • the length of any probationary period; • the overall purpose of the post; • the main duties and responsibilities of the post; and • the individual's responsibility for promoting and safeguarding the welfare of children s/he is responsible for, or comes into contact with. The person specification is the key tool for successful recruitment. This provides potential applicants with information about what they will need to demonstrate to show their ability to undertake a particular role and provides the basis for short-listing candidates. It also provides your interview panel with the selection criteria by which to assess the best candidate for the role. The person specification should be completed in a consistent template for the organisation and should clearly state: • the skills and abilities, knowledge, experience and qualifications needed to perform the role in relation to working with children; • the essential competences and qualities that the successful candidate must be able to demonstrate (including at a minimum the ability to safeguard the welfare of children); • any other desirable competences and qualities that are not essential but would help someone perform the role; and • how these requirements will be tested and assessed during the selection process. The person specification should clearly indicate which criteria are 'essential' for the appointment of the preferred candidate and which criteria are 'desirable' through which the candidate may demonstrate additional experience, skills or qualifications that may assist with the post. The person specification should also indicate how the candidates can expect each of the criteria to be assessed (i.e. through the application form, at interview, with a test or exercise or other alternative form of assessment).

These notes have been compiled from a variety of sources outlining best practice and provide background to the safer recruitment audit	
BEFORE DETAILS OF POST ARE RELEASED	
Step 4: **Advertisement**	The advertisement should include a statement about the employer's commitment to safeguarding and promoting the welfare of children. You should also highlight the need for the successful applicant to undertake vetting checks, including Enhanced DBS and Barred list check.

These notes have been compiled from a variety of sources outlining best practice and provide background to the safer recruitment audit.

BEFORE DETAILS OF POST ARE RELEASED

Step 5: Candidate information pack & application form (Part 1)	Use a standard application form to obtain a common set of information from all applicants. It is not good practice to accept curriculum vitae drawn up by applicants in place of an application form because these will only contain the information the applicant wishes to present and may omit relevant details. The essential information requested on all application forms should include: • full identifying details of the applicant including current and former names, date of birth, current address and National Insurance number; • a statement of any academic and/or vocational qualifications the applicant has obtained that are relevant to the position for which s/he is applying with details of the awarding body and date of award; • relevant registration information and reference numbers for posts requiring professional registration.; • a full career and education history in chronological order since leaving secondary education, including periods of any post-secondary education or training, part-time and voluntary work as well as full-time employment. Start and end dates, explanations for periods not in employment, education or training, and reasons for leaving employment should also be provided; • a declaration of any family or close relationship to existing employees or employers (including councillors, company directors or trustees); • details of at least two referees. One referee should be the applicant's current or most recent employer and, wherever possible, at least one of them should be able to comment on the applicant's work with children. All referees should be asked about the candidate's suitability for the role in question and whether the referee knows any reason why the applicant should not work with children. Where an applicant is not currently working with children, but has done so in the past, it is good practice that a reference is also obtained from the last employer for whom the person was employed in work with children. Where an applicant has not worked in a paid capacity previously (e.g. school or college leaver or placement student) references from their latest or current educational establishment, any voluntary work or, in exceptional cases, someone who knows the candidate well from other activities are acceptable. The application form should make it clear that references will not be accepted from relatives; • a statement giving examples of how the applicant can demonstrate they meet the competences, personal qualities, skills, and expertise within the person specification as essential for the role and any additional qualities that are specified as desirable. The application form should also include a brief explanation that the post is exempt from the Rehabilitation of Offenders Act 1974 and ask the candidate to declare whether s/he has any convictions, cautions and bind-overs, including any that would normally be regarded as 'spent'. If the declaration is positive, details must be provided on the application form.

These notes have been compiled from a variety of sources outlining best practice and provide background to the safer recruitment audit.

BEFORE DETAILS OF POST ARE RELEASED

Step 5: **Candidate information pack & application form (Part 2)**	The application form should also require a signed statement that the person is not disqualified from work with children, or subject to sanctions imposed by a regulatory or professional body.
	All applicants should also be informed that:
	• the successful applicant will be required to undergo the required vetting checks. As a minimum, Enhanced DBS with Barred List check.
	• you will seek references on short listed candidates that will include questions about past disciplinary actions or allegations in relation to behaviour with children, and may approach previous employers for information to verify particular experience or qualifications, before interview (you may wish to provide applicants with a contact number so that they can discuss this if they have concerns about it);
	• providing false information is an offence and could result in the application being rejected or summary dismissal if the applicant has been selected and possible referral to the police and/or DBS.

These notes have been compiled from a variety of sources outlining best practice and provide background to the safer recruitment audit.

BEFORE DETAILS OF POST ARE RELEASED

Step 5: **Candidate information pack & application form** **(Part 3)**	The candidate information pack is one of your first opportunities to present a good, professional impression to potential applicants. It is also the best chance to provide your applicants with all the information they may need to submit an application that could result in them being short-listed for interview. You should consider whether you wish to standardise the information that is provided in all packs for posts working with children. At the very least, your pack should include: • an introductory letter explaining the purpose of the post, its significance to or position within the organisation and any significant dates in relation to the recruitment process (i.e. closing date for applications, short listing and interviews); • the application form, explanatory notes about completing the form, and information about how candidates with a disability, or for whom English is not their first language, can get help to complete the form; • the job description and person specification; and • the organisation's child protection and/or safeguarding policy statement.

These notes have been compiled from a variety of sources outlining best practice and provide background to the safer recruitment audit.

BEFORE AN INTERVIEW

Step 6: **Scrutiny of application forms**	Each application should be scrutinised by the appointed short-listing panel to make sure: • they are fully and properly completed; and • the information provided is consistent, does not contain any discrepancies and any gaps in employment are identified. The short-listing panel should consist of at least two people, preferably members of the interview panel, who should meet and undertake the task together. Any applications that are significantly incomplete should not be accepted or short-listed. Any anomalies, discrepancies or gaps in employment identified by the scrutiny should be taken into account in considering whether to short-list the applicant. As well as reasons for obvious gaps in employment, the reasons for a history of repeated changes of employment without any clear career or salary progression, or a mid-career move from a permanent post to agency, freelance or temporary work, also need to be explored and confirmed. Following the above checks, you should assess each application that is received in relation to whether the required criteria have been demonstrably met by the applicant in his/her application form. This may not be all the criteria from the person specification, but just the key criteria you have identified on the person specification. All candidates should be assessed equally against the same criteria without exception or variation and agreement reached by your short-listing panel about which applicants to invite for interview. The panel should record its decision about each application, in case of queries afterwards. Using a system where applicants are scored or rated against each of the short-listing criteria will help you to demonstrate that decisions were objective and without prejudice if necessary.

BEFORE AN INTERVIEW

Step 7: References	References should always be sought and obtained directly from the referee and not through a third party or the candidate themselves (one of which should be the applicant's current employer). All posts should be subject to the taking up of references as this is an indispensable tool within the safer recruitment process. In all cases you should obtain at least two references to provide both professional and personal perspectives on the candidate and his/her ability, motivation and aptitude for the post. Written references should be obtained directly from the referee and addressed to the chair of your interview panel or recruitment agency. References supplied by an applicant or addressed in any other way, i.e. 'To Whom It May Concern' should not be accepted. It is acceptable to follow the receipt of a written reference with a telephone call to confirm its authenticity. Reference requests should be accompanied by a copy of the job description and person specification asking for the following: • the referee's relationship with the candidate; • details of current post; • sick record; • specific comments about the applicant's suitability for the post, including performance history and conduct; • details of any disciplinary procedures the applicant has been subject to in which the disciplinary sanction is current; • details of any allegations, concerns or disciplinary procedures that have been raised about the applicant that relate to the safety and welfare of children, young people or vulnerable adults and the outcome of those concerns/proceedings; and • whether the referee is completely satisfied that the candidate is suitable to work with children and , if not, specific details of the referee's concerns and the reasons why the referee believes the person may be unsuitable. If the applicant is not currently employed in a role directly with children or young people, checks need to be undertaken with their last employer in this type of role. If references do not provide the detail necessary to verify all the above points, the referee should be contacted and asked to expand on answers to ensure that you have all the information necessary to make a decision. All information provided on references should be correlated with information provided on the application form.

These notes have been compiled from a variety of sources outlining best practice and provide background to the safer recruitment audit.

BEFORE AN INTERVIEW

Step 8: **Invitation for interview**	The letter inviting candidates to interview should provide them with the following: • time and venue; • directions to the venue; • membership of the interview panel; • any specific task that has been set to assist in the selection process and the time/method allocated for this; • the selection process (i.e. an objective scoring system based on the criteria within the person specification); • information about any specific areas of exploration, including suitability to work with children, and any issues arising from the candidate's references or disclosure of criminal background; and • to inform you of any special requirements (e.g. access, large print/Braille, interpreters). The invitation should also stress that you will need to check and confirm the identity of the successful candidate thoroughly to ensure the person is who he or she claims to be. Where an Enhanced DBS disclosure is appropriate you may wish to ask the person to complete an application for a DBS disclosure straight away. You should ask all candidates to bring with them documentary evidence of their identity that will satisfy DBS requirements. This means that the application for the successful candidate can be processed immediately. If you have specified that candidates will need to hold specific qualification for the post, you will need to ask them to bring any documents confirming their educational and professional qualifications that are necessary or relevant for the post, e.g. the original or a certified copy of a certificate, diploma or degree or a letter of confirmation from the awarding body. Note: If the successful candidate cannot produce original documents or certified copies, written confirmation of his or her relevant qualifications must be obtained from the awarding body. A copy of the documents used to verify the successful candidate's identity and qualifications must be kept for your personnel records.

BEFORE SELECTING A PREFERED CANDIDATE

Step 9: **Interview**	In addition to assessing the candidate's ability to perform the duties of the post, the interview will also explore issues relating to safeguarding and promoting the welfare of children including: • motivation to work with children and young people; • ability to form and maintain appropriate relationships and personal boundaries with children and young people; • emotional resilience in working with challenging behaviours; • attitudes to use of authority and maintaining discipline; and • explain that if the applicant is short-listed any relevant issues arising from his or her references will be taken up at interview. The interview should assess each candidate against the selection criteria derived from the job description and person specification, and explore their suitability to work with children. Interviews should also be seen as an opportunity for you to get the best from the candidates and provide them with the chance to demonstrate how they meet the specification for the role – it should not be seen as a test where no assistance can be provided or where candidates should feel they might be caught out by trick questions. The selection process for people who will work with children should always include a face-to-face interview even if there is only one candidate. It is good practice for your interview panel to have a minimum of two interviewers. A panel of at least two people allows one member to observe and assess the candidate and make notes, while the candidate is talking to the other. It also reduces the possibility of any dispute about what was said or asked during the interview. All panel members should familiarise themselves with the candidates application forms prior to the interviews starting. The members of the panel should: • have the necessary authority to make decisions about appointment; • be appropriately experienced or trained; and • meet before the interviews to (i) reach agreement about the required standard (or scoring threshold if being used) for the job to which they are appointing, (ii) consider the issues to be explored with each candidate and who will ask about each of those, and (iii) agree their selection criteria in accordance with the person specification, the method of assessment they will use and the standards they will apply.

These notes have been compiled from a variety of sources outlining best practice and provide background to the safer recruitment audit.

BEFORE SELECTING A PREFERED CANDIDATE

Step 9: Interview (continued)	The panel will need to agree a set of questions they will ask all candidates relating to the requirements of the post, and the issues they will explore with each, based on the information provided in the applications and references (if available). If the applicant has declared any past criminal convictions the panel will also need to consider whether those are relevant and whether they raise issues that need to be explored with the candidate at interview. Guidance about assessing the relevance of criminal record information and the Rehabilitation of Offenders Act, 1974 can be found on the DBS website. How you assess and follow up a question or issue at interview will depend on the candidate's responses. Where possible it is best to avoid hypothetical questions because they allow theoretical answers. It is better to ask competence or value-based questions that ask a candidate to relate how they responded to or dealt with an actual situation, or questions that test their attitudes and understanding of issues. If a scoring mechanism is to be used to assess suitability against each of the criteria, this should be clearly explained to the candidates. This could simply be: 1 = demonstrates no understanding/competence 2 = demonstrates some understanding/competence 3 = demonstrates reasonable understanding/competence 4 = demonstrates good understanding/competence 5 = demonstrates excellent understanding/competence

These notes have been compiled from a variety of sources outlining best practice and provide background to the safer recruitment audit.

BEFORE SELECTING A PREFERED CANDIDATE

Step 10: Suitability of questions	In addition to assessing and evaluating the applicant's suitability for a post using the person specification criteria, the interview panel should also explore: • the candidate's attitude towards children; • his or her ability to support the organisation's commitment to safeguarding and promoting the welfare of children; • gaps in the candidate's employment history; • concerns or discrepancies arising from the information provided by the candidate and/or a referee; and • issues arising from any disclosure of a criminal record by the applicant. The panel should also ask the candidate if they wish to add anything to the declaration on their application form in light of the requirement for a Enhanced DBS disclosure with barred list check. If, for whatever reason, you have been unable to obtain references before the interview, the candidate should also be asked at interview if there is anything s/he wishes to declare or discuss in light of the questions that have been (or will be) put to his or her referees. It is vital that you obtain and scrutinise the references and resolve any issues satisfactorily before you confirm appointment and before s/he starts work.

These notes have been compiled from a variety of sources outlining best practice and provide background to the safer recruitment audit.

BEFORE APPOINTING FORMALLY

Step 11: **Confident selection**	Panel is confident that the candidate being offered the job can meet the requirement of the post to the desired level and that there are no safeguarding concerns.
Step 12: **Confirmation in writing**	An offer of appointment to the successful candidate can be made, but the offer must be conditional on the satisfactory completion of the vetting checks, including: • the receipt of at least two satisfactory references; • verification of the candidate's identity (if that could not be verified straight after the interview); • appropriate vetting checks and DBS disclosure; • verification of qualifications (if not verified at the interview); • verification of professional status where required All checks should be: • confirmed in writing; • documented and retained in a secure place (subject to relevant advice contained in the DBS Code of Practice and the Data Protection Act, 1998); • followed-up where they are unsatisfactory or there are discrepancies in the information provided. The details of checks must be reported to the police and/or the DBS if: • the DBS disclosure shows s/he has been disqualified from working with children; • an applicant has provided false information in, or in support of, his or her application; • there are serious concerns about an applicant's suitability to work with children gained from other legitimate information sources (e.g. references). DBS disclosures must be completed on overseas staff. In addition, criminal records information (or certificates of good conduct) should be sought from countries where individuals have worked or lived.

Safer recruitment audit

Strand	Point to check	Evidence	Actions (if necessary)
Policy	Recruitment and selection policy in place.		
Commitment	Commitment to safeguarding included on: o publicity materials o adverts and recruitment websites o candidate information packs o job descriptions and person specs o induction training arrangements.		
Process Planning	Timetable for recruitment process is planned to allow references to be obtained on short-listed candidates before the interview.		
	Job description and person specification clearly defined, including safeguarding requirements of the post.		
Advert	Advert refers to safeguarding commitment and that safeguarding checks will be undertaken.		

Strand	Point to check	Evidence	Actions (if necessary)
Candidate information pack and application form	Standard application form is used allowing all candidates to submit consistent information (unless the applicant has a disability preventing them from completing the application form).		
	Information sent to candidates includes clear safeguarding statement.		
Scrutiny of application forms	Short-listing panel scrutinise applications using scoring/rating system against agreed criteria.		
References	Two references sought and obtained directly from the referee prior to interview.		
	Open references not accepted.		
	Written references are subject to verification and follow up.		
	References routinely include reference to suitability to work with children and young people; whether there are concerns about working with the age group; referees relationship to candidate; whether they have knowledge that the candidate has ever been investigated over safeguarding issues.		

Strand	Point to check	Evidence	Actions (if necessary)
Invitation to interview	Standard invitation to interview outlines how safeguarding will feature, e.g. through identity checks and questioning.		
Interview	Interviews are face to face with minimum of two people; one of whom must have undertaken safer recruitment training.		
	Safeguarding questions included in interview		
	Gaps in employment are checked.		
	Concerns and/or discrepancies in information provided by candidate and/or referee are explored thoroughly.		
	Candidates are routinely asked if they wish to declare anything in light of the requirement for thorough vetting checks (may be included on the application form).		
Confirm-ation	All offers confirmed in writing stating checks to be undertaken.		
Vetting	Vetting checks in place (see SCR checklist)		

Glossary

Glossary

Barred	Anyone barred by the DBS from working with children (or vulnerable adults) breaks the law if they seek that type of work. Some people are barred automatically on conviction of specific serious offences; others are barred after being dismissed from their role for a child protection incident. People barred from working with children are not barred from volunteering with children as long as they are not in regulated activity.
DBS	Disclosure & Barring Service – previously the Criminal Record Bureau (CRB), it amalgamated with the Independent Safeguarding Authority (ISA) in 2010.
DBS barred list check	A check of the list of people barred from working in regulated activity with children in England. There is also a separate list of people barred from working with adults Schools are required by law to check that a new recruit is not barred before the person commences in post.
DBS certificate	A document that lists any relevant criminal convictions, cautions or bind-overs a person has accrued. Used by employers to determine suitability for certain employment Schools must by law undertake an enhanced DBS certificate for any new staff (and some other adults) unless there is an exemption.
List 99	No longer exists. It was previously the list of people barred from working in schools but has been replaced by the DBS barred list.
NCTL	National College of Teaching & Leadership – an amalgamation of the National College of School Leadership (NCSL) and General Teaching Council (GTC). Leads on Teacher Standards and professional development of teachers / school leaders.
NCTL Prohibited list	The list of teachers prohibited as a result of misconduct. There is also an interim prohibition list for teachers accused of serious criminal offences. Since 02/09/2013 schools are required by law to check that any newly appointed teacher with QTS is not prohibited
Prohibition	Teachers can be prohibited from teaching (i.e. have their QTS removed) as a result of serious misconduct, failure to meet the standards required of a teacher or for bringing the profession into disrepute.
QTS	Qualified Teacher Status
Regulated activity	Work that barred people must not do. Includes teaching, training, coaching, being employed in a school or children's home, child-minding, etc but does not apply to supervised volunteers.